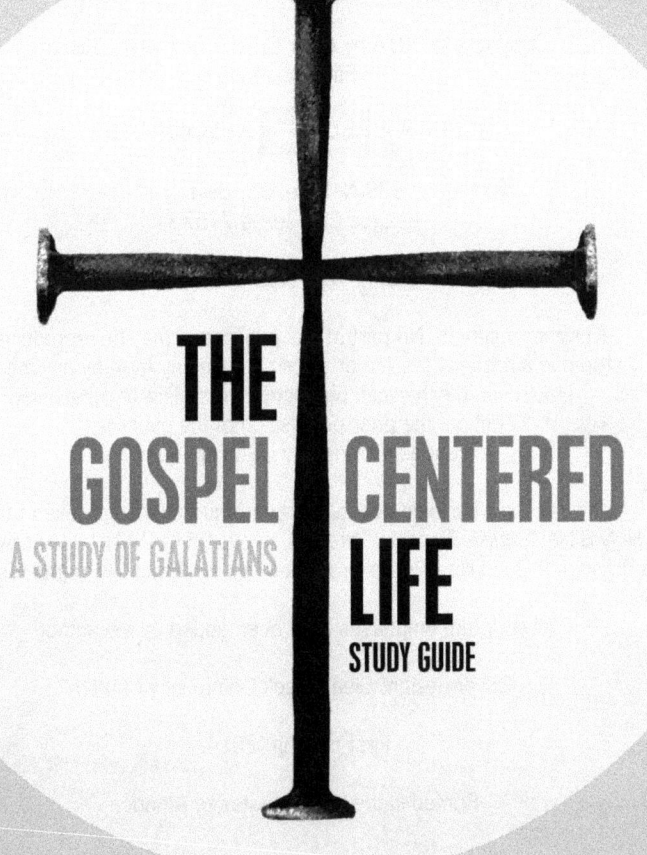

The Gospel-Centered Life: A Study of Galatians (Study Guide)

Copyright © 2014 by Clear Creek Community Church
Published by:

CLEAR CREEK RESOURCES

999 N. Egret Bay Blvd.
League City, Texas 77573

ISBN 978-0-9825517-6-9

All rights reserved. No part of this publication may be reproduced,
stored in a retrieval system or transmitted in any form by any means,
electronic, mechanical, photocopy, recording or otherwise,
without the prior permission of the publisher,
except as provided by USA copyright law.

Unless otherwise indicated, all Scripture quotations are taken from:
The Holy Bible: English Standard Version®, copyright © 2001 by Crossway Bibles,
a division of Good New Publishers. Used by permission. All rights reserved.

All scripture emphases have been added by the author.

Cover design: Clear Creek Community Church

First printing, 2014.

Printed in the United States of America

CONTENTS

SESSION 1: The Gospel is Good News, Not Good Advice.
Galatians 1:1-9
Video Clip: "The Greatness of the Gospel"

SESSION 2: Grace Always Takes the Initiative.
Galatians 1:10-24
Video Clip: "How Grace Works"

SESSION 3: The Good Fight is Christ Alone vs. Christ Plus or Minus Anything.
Galatians 2:1-10
Video Clip: "The Good Fight" [Two video clips]

SESSION 4: Justification: God's Act of Declaring Sinners Righteous!
Galatians 2:11-21
Video Clip: "Living the Gospel"

SESSION 5: The Righteous Shall Live By Faith.
Galatians 3:1-14
Video Clip: "Just By Faith"

SESSION 6: The Good News About the Law is That It Points You to Jesus.
Galatians 3:15-25
Video Clip: "The Good News About Law"

SESSION 7: We Have a New Status in Christ.
Galatians 3:26-4:7
Video Clip: "From Slaves to Sons"

SESSION 8: Catch Your Drift with Gospel-Centered Relationships and Teaching.
Galatians 4:8-31
Video Clip: "Catching Your Drift" [Two video clips]

SESSION 9: The Way You Experience God Determines the Way People Experience You.
Galatians 5:1-15
Video Clip: "The Free Way"

SESSION 10: Belief Determines Behavior.
Galatians 5:16-26
Video Clip: "By the Spirit"

SESSION 11: How You See Yourself Determines How You Treat Others.
Galatians 5:26-6:5
Video Clip: "Gospel Relationships"

SESSION 12: We Reap What We Sow.
Galatians 6:6-18
Video Clip: "The Gospel and the Harvest"

Dear Group Member:

Welcome to *The Gospel-Centered Life: A Study of Galatians*. We hope this study guide helps you both dig into the book of Galatians and prepare you for group discussion. You will notice that each small group session is structured to help you develop good Bible study habits by intentionally following a three-step pattern:

1) *Observation* (WHAT does this passage say?)

2) *Interpretation* (WHAT does this passage mean?)

3. *Application* (HOW do I apply this passage to my life?).

In order to make the most of your small group experience, please read the assigned text each week at least three times and answer the respective questions. The *Group Reading* and *Group Notes* sections are to be done during your small group gathering.

So, jump in! Learn and grow in the glorious gospel of Jesus!

– The Elders of Clear Creek Community Church

SESSION 1

{ THE GOSPEL IS GOOD NEWS, NOT GOOD ADVICE. }

GALATIANS 1:1-9

¹Paul, an apostle – not from men nor through man, but through Jesus Christ and God the Father, who raised him from the dead – ²and all the brothers who are with me,
To the churches of Galatia:
³Grace to you and peace from God our Father and the Lord Jesus Christ, ⁴who gave himself for our sins to deliver us from the present evil age, according to the will of our God and Father, ⁵to whom be the glory forever and ever. Amen.
⁶I am astonished that you are so quickly deserting him who called you in the grace of Christ and are turning to a different gospel – ⁷not that there is another one, but there are some who trouble you and want to distort the gospel of Christ. ⁸But even if we or an angel from heaven should preach to you a gospel contrary to the one we preached to you, let him be accursed. ⁹As we have said before, so now I say again: If anyone is preaching to you a gospel contrary to the one you received, let him be accursed.

REFLECTION:
Read through Galatians 1:1-9 at least three times this week. Each day make notes of any thoughts and observations and answer the questions provided.

DAY 1:
_____
_____
_____
_____
_____
_____

SESSION 1 • The Gospel is Good News, Not Good Advice.

(vv. 1-2) Who wrote this letter and to whom? _____
_____

(vv. 1-9) List everyone mentioned in this text. _____
_____
_____
_____

DAY 2:

_____
_____
_____
_____
_____

(v. 3) In the first half of verse 3 Paul greets the Galatians with two words which hold a great message and blessing. What are they? _____
_____

DAY 3:

_____
_____
_____
_____
_____

(vv. 6-9) What is the problem Paul describes? _____
_____
_____
_____

GROUP READING: HISTORY

The apostle Paul traveled and preached the gospel of Jesus Christ throughout the ancient Near East and Asia Minor, including Galatia, where, by the work of the Holy Spirit, many people became Christians and churches were established. However, the Galatian churches soon were infiltrated by "Judaizers" whose false teaching included the addition of Jewish customs and rituals as requirements to be a Christian. Essentially, the Judaizers said the gospel alone was insufficient. Paul wrote this letter to help the Galatians understand and accept the gospel, faith alone in Jesus Christ alone, as the only true gospel.

GROUP NOTES:

SESSION 2

{ GRACE ALWAYS TAKES THE INITIATIVE. }

GALATIANS 1:10-24

¹⁰ Am I now trying to win the approval of human beings, or of God? Or am I trying to please people? If I were still trying to please people, I would not be a servant of Christ.

¹¹ I want you to know, brothers and sisters, that the gospel I preached is not of human origin. ¹² I did not receive it from any man, nor was I taught it; rather, I received it by revelation from Jesus Christ.

¹³ For you have heard of my previous way of life in Judaism, how intensely I persecuted the church of God and tried to destroy it. ¹⁴ I was advancing in Judaism beyond many of my own age among my people and was extremely zealous for the traditions of my fathers. ¹⁵ But when God, who set me apart from my mother's womb and called me by his grace, was pleased ¹⁶ to reveal his Son in me so that I might preach him among the Gentiles, my immediate response was not to consult any human being. ¹⁷ I did not go up to Jerusalem to see those who were apostles before I was, but I went into Arabia. Later I returned to Damascus.

¹⁸ Then after three years, I went up to Jerusalem to get acquainted with Cephas and stayed with him fifteen days. ¹⁹ I saw none of the other apostles—only James, the Lord's brother. ²⁰ I assure you before God that what I am writing you is no lie.

²¹ Then I went to Syria and Cilicia. ²² I was personally unknown to the churches of Judea that are in Christ. ²³ They only heard the report: "The man who formerly persecuted us is now preaching the faith he once tried to destroy." ²⁴ And they praised God because of me.

SESSION 2 • Grace Always Takes the Initiative.

REFLECTION:
Read through Galatians 1:10-24 at least three times this week. Each day make notes of any thoughts and observations and answer the questions provided.

DAY 1:
_____
_____
_____
_____
_____
_____

(vv. 13-14) What words describe Paul's previous life? _____
_____
_____

DAY 2:
_____
_____
_____
_____
_____

(vv. 13-16) What positive thing(s) did Paul do to please God in these verses? What did God do? (vv. 13-16) _____
_____
_____

DAY 3:
_____
_____
_____
_____
_____

\(vv. 21-24) What was the report the churches of v. 22 heard about Paul? What was their response? _____
_____
_____

SESSION 2

GROUP READING: INTRODUCTION

The apostle Paul firmly established the Galatian churches with the message of a grace-given gospel but later found them contaminated by the Judaizers, false teachers who attempted to discredit Paul and proclaim his gospel incomplete. Paul, passionate about reclaiming the church with the true gospel, shared the grace-filled story of his past and his present as an expanded response to the Judaizers' lies. His rebuttal of their accusations showed how grace worked in his life and, consequently, how it works in ours.

GROUP NOTES:

SESSION 3

{THE GOOD FIGHT IS CHRIST ALONE VS. CHRIST PLUS OR MINUS ANYTHING.}

GALATIANS 2:1-10

¹Then, after fourteen years I went up again to Jerusalem with Barnabas, taking Titus along with me. ²I went up because of a revelation and set before them (though privately before those who seemed influential) the gospel that I proclaim among the Gentiles, in order to make sure I was not running or had not run in vain. ³But even Titus, who was with me, was not forced to be circumcised, though he was a Greek. ⁴Yet because of false brothers secretly brought in—who slipped in to spy out our freedom that we have in Christ Jesus, so that they might bring us into slavery— ⁵to them we did not yield in submission even for a moment, so that the truth of the gospel might be preserved for you. ⁶And from those who seemed to be influential (what they were makes no difference to me; God shows no partiality)—those, I say, who seemed influential added nothing to me. ⁷On the contrary, when they saw that I had been entrusted with the gospel to the uncircumcised, just as Peter had been entrusted with the gospel to the circumcised ⁸(for he who worked through Peter for his apostolic ministry to the circumcised worked also through me for mine to the Gentiles), ⁹and when James and Cephas and John, who seemed to be pillars, perceived the grace that was given to me, they gave the right hand of fellowship to Barnabas and me, that we should go to the Gentiles and they to the circumcised. ¹⁰Only, they asked us to remember the poor, the very thing I was eager to do.

REFLECTION:
Read through Galatians 2:1-10 at least three times this week. Each day make notes of any thoughts and observations and answer the questions provided.

SESSION 3 • The Good Fight is Christ Alone vs. Christ Plus or Minus Anything.

DAY 1:

_____
_____
_____
_____
_____

(vv. 1-10) List all of the people mentioned in this text. _____
_____
_____

DAY 2:

_____
_____
_____
_____
_____

vv. 1-3) Where did Paul go and who went with him? What does the text say about Titus? _____
_____
_____

DAY 3:

_____
_____
_____
_____
_____

(vv. 7-8) Paul and Peter were entrusted with two different ministries. What were they? _____
_____
_____

GROUP READING: INTRODUCTION

In his letter to the Galatians, Paul wrote that the gospel is news and grace (Christ alone, as opposed to Christ plus or minus anything). In this week's text he showed himself willing to fight for the gospel that he saw being threatened. Fourteen years after his first visit to Jerusalem, Paul returned to meet with some of the most influential Christian leaders. He brought with him Barnabas and Titus, an uncircumcised Greek Christian, in what appeared to be a test to see if these Jewish Christian leaders would hold true to the gospel, the gospel of Christ alone.

GROUP NOTES:

SESSION 4

{ JUSTIFICATION: GOD'S ACT OF DECLARING SINNERS RIGHTEOUS! }

GALATIANS 2:11-21

¹¹But when Cephas came to Antioch, I opposed him to his face, because he stood condemned. ¹²For before certain men came from James, he was eating with the Gentiles; but when they came he drew back and separated himself, fearing the circumcision party. ¹³And the rest of the Jews acted hypocritically along with him, so that even Barnabas was led astray by their hypocrisy. ¹⁴But when I saw that their conduct was not in step with the truth of the gospel, I said to Cephas before them all, "If you, though a Jew, live like a Gentile and not like a Jew, how can you force the Gentiles to live like Jews? "

¹⁵We ourselves are Jews by birth and not Gentile sinners; ¹⁶yet we know that a person is not justified by works of the law but through faith in Jesus Christ, so we also have believed in Christ Jesus, in order to be justified by faith in Christ and not by works of the law, because by works of the law no one will be justified.

¹⁷But if, in our endeavor to be justified in Christ, we too were found to be sinners, is Christ then a servant of sin? Certainly not! ¹⁸For if I rebuild what I tore down, I prove myself to be a transgressor. ¹⁹For through the law I died to the law, so that I might live to God. ²⁰I have been crucified with Christ. It is no longer I who live, but Christ who lives in me. And the life I now live in the flesh I live by faith in the Son of God, who loved me and gave himself for me. ²¹ I do not nullify the grace of God, for if righteousness were through the law, then Christ died for no purpose.

REFLECTION:
Read through Galatians 2:11-21 at least three times this week. Each day make notes of any thoughts and observations and answer the questions provided.

SESSION 4 • Justification: God's Act of Declaring Sinners Righteous!

DAY 1:

(vv. 11-14) What did Peter (Cephas) do in these verses and what was Paul's response? _____

DAY 2:

(v. 13) How did Peter's behavior influence Barnabas? _____

DAY 3:

(vv. 15-21) To "justify" is to declare someone not guilty; innocent or righteous. How many times is the word "justified" used in these verses? _____

GROUP READING: BACK STORY

The church began primarily as a Jewish-flavored community. After all, Jesus was the Jewish Messiah, the apostles were all Jews, and the church was born in the midst of the Jewish Pentecost celebration in the most Jewish of all cities, Jerusalem. The first gospel message was by Peter to Jews and the first church of 3,000 men and women was established with a definitely Jewish feel. These new believers experienced life together, including the practice of attending temple. After all, they were Jews. But the world that Jesus came to save was bigger than simply the Jewish Jerusalem, and the farther you moved from Jerusalem, the less Jewish the world became. God's plan was to save, not only Jews, but people from every tribe and nation.

GROUP NOTES:

SESSION 5

{ THE RIGHTEOUS SHALL LIVE BY FAITH. }

GALATIANS 3:1-14

¹⁰ O foolish Galatians! Who has bewitched you? It was before your eyes that Jesus Christ was publicly portrayed as crucified. ²Let me ask you only this: Did you receive the Spirit by works of the law or by hearing with faith? ³Are you so foolish? Having begun by the Spirit, are you now being perfected by the flesh? ⁴ Did you suffer so many things in vain—if indeed it was in vain? ⁵Does he who supplies the Spirit to you and works miracles among you do so by works of the law, or by hearing with faith— ⁶just as Abraham "believed God, and it was counted to him as righteousness?"

⁷Know then that it is those of faith who are the sons of Abraham. ⁸And the Scripture, foreseeing that God would justify the Gentiles by faith, preached the gospel beforehand to Abraham, saying, "In you shall all the nations be blessed." ⁹So then, those who are of faith are blessed along with Abraham, the man of faith.

¹⁰For all who rely on works of the law are under a curse; for it is written, "Cursed be everyone who does not abide by all things written in the Book of the Law, and do them." ¹¹Now it is evident that no one is justified before God by the law, for "The righteous shall live by faith." ¹²But the law is not of faith, rather "The one who does them shall live by them." ¹³Christ redeemed us from the curse of the law by becoming a curse for us—for it is written, "Cursed is everyone who is hanged on a tree" — ¹⁴so that in Christ Jesus the blessing of Abraham might come to the Gentiles, so that we might receive the promised Spirit through faith.

REFLECTION:
Read through Galatians 3:1-14 at least three times this week. Each day make notes of any thoughts and observations and answer the questions provided.

SESSION 5 • The Righteous Shall Live by Faith.

DAY 1:

_____
_____
_____
_____
_____

(vv. 1-6) Paul asks several questions. What are they? _____
_____

DAY 2:

_____
_____
_____
_____

(vv. 7-9) Circle each time you see the word "faith." What does Paul say about faith and those who have it? _____
_____

DAY 3:

_____
_____
_____
_____
_____

(vv. 10-14) Circle each time you see the word "law." What does Paul say about the law and those who rely on it? _____
_____

GROUP READING: INTRODUCTION

Paul already made the case that the gospel was good news we received by grace. The gospel, our hope of justification, was threatened and worthy of being defended. In this text, Paul asked questions of the Galatians, the first of which was, "Who has bewitched you?" Such an interesting way to begin. He almost asked, "Why are you so stupid?" before going on to write about how clearly they originally received the gospel. Paul compared a life lived by faith to one lived by law and in the process showed a clearer picture of faith as reflected in the life of Abraham.

GROUP NOTES:

SESSION 6

{ THE GOOD NEWS ABOUT THE LAW IS THAT IT POINTS YOU TO JESUS. }

GALATIANS 3:15-25

¹⁵ To give a human example, brothers: even with a man-made covenant, no one annuls it or adds to it once it has been ratified. ¹⁶Now the promises were made to Abraham and to his offspring. It does not say, "And to offsprings," referring to many, but referring to one, "And to your offspring," who is Christ. ¹⁷This is what I mean: the law, which came 430 years afterward, does not annul a covenant previously ratified by God, so as to make the promise void. ¹⁸For if the inheritance comes by the law, it no longer comes by promise; but God gave it to Abraham by a promise.

¹⁹ Why then the law? It was added because of transgressions, until the offspring should come to whom the promise had been made, and it was put in place through angels by an intermediary. ²⁰Now an intermediary implies more than one, but God is one.

²¹Is the law then contrary to the promises of God? Certainly not! For if a law had been given that could give life, then righteousness would indeed be by the law. ²²But the Scripture imprisoned everything under sin, so that the promise by faith in Jesus Christ might be given to those who believe.

²³Now before faith came, we were held captive under the law, imprisoned until the coming faith would be revealed. ²⁴So then, the law was our guardian until Christ came, in order that we might be justified by faith. ²⁵But now that faith has come, we are no longer under a guardian, we might receive the promised Spirit through faith.

REFLECTION:
Read through Galatians 3:15-25 at least three times this week. Each day make notes of any thoughts and observations and answer the questions provided.

SESSION 6 • The Good News About the Law is That it Points You to Jesus.

DAY 1:

_____

(vv. 1-6) Paul asks several questions. What are they? _____

DAY 2:

_____

(vv. 17-18) Circle the words "promise" and "inheritance." What did Paul say here about the promise and the inheritance? _____

DAY 3:

_____

(vv. 19-25) These verses describe the purpose for the law and end with a word that describes the role of the law. It's used twice in v. 24 and 25. What is it? _____

GROUP READING: BACKGROUND
God gave to Abraham a promise of the Messiah to come. The Jews took this promise to be about the real estate they would call Israel, the Promised Land, but Paul said the promise had a greater fulfillment, in Jesus. Ultimately God's promise is not to bring his people within the borders of a city limit somewhere, but into the promised land of his kingdom where we are redeemed by faith in Jesus alone.

God's promise to Abraham is that anyone can come into the promised land of his kingdom, but they must believe by faith in Jesus for what he's done and who he is.

Even in the days of the Old Testament, salvation did not come by an individual's moral performance, but by faith placed in the promised Messiah to come. Entrance into God's kingdom has NEVER been about someone's ability to obey God's law because no one can do it perfectly, except Jesus.

Galatians 3:15-25 gives a look into the promise given to Abraham and eventually to us.

GROUP NOTES:

SESSION 6 • The Good News About the Law is That it Points You to Jesus.

___

Leash   List   Lense   Ladder

PROMISE　　　　　　　PERFORMANCE
FAITH　　　　　　　　LAW
GRATITUDE　　　　　　GUILT
THANKFUL　　　　　　OBLIGATION
GOSPEL　　　　　　　RELIGION
SAVES　　　　　　　　CONDEMNS
HEAVEN　　　　　　　NO HEAVEN
GOD: "I WILL"　　　　　GOD: "YOU WILL"
CHRISTIAN　　　　　　JUDAIZER

SESSION 7

{ WE HAVE A NEW STATUS IN CHRIST. }

GALATIANS 3:26-4:7

26for in Christ Jesus you are all sons of God, through faith. 27For as many of you as were baptized into Christ have put on Christ. 28There is neither Jew nor Greek, there is neither slave nor free, there is no male and female, for you are all one in Christ Jesus. 29And if you are Christ's, then you are Abraham's offspring, heirs according to promise.

1I mean that the heir, as long as he is a child, is no different from a slave, though he is the owner of everything, 2but he is under guardians and managers until the date set by his father. 3In the same way we also, when we were children, were enslaved to the elementary principles of the world. 4But when the fullness of time had come, God sent forth his Son, born of woman, born under the law, 5to redeem those who were under the law, so that we might receive adoption as sons. 6And because you are sons, God has sent the Spirit of his Son into our hearts, crying, "Abba! Father!" 7So you are no longer a slave, but a son, and if a son, then an heir through God.

REFLECTION:
Read through Galatians 3:26-4:7 at least three times this week. Each day make notes of any thoughts and observations and answer the questions provided.

SESSION 7 • We Have a New Status In Christ.

DAY 1:

_____
_____
_____
_____
_____
_____

(v. 26) Through faith in Christ Jesus we are changed to become what? _____
_____
_____

DAY 2:

_____
_____
_____
_____
_____
_____

(v. 28) As believers, our identity has changed and we belong to Jesus Christ, we are Abraham's offspring and heirs. All of this comes according to what?
_____
_____

DAY 3:

_____
_____
_____
_____
_____
_____

(vv. 4-5) Paul says God sent forth his son for what purpose? _____
_____
_____

GROUP READING: INTRODUCTION
The blockbuster movie called "The Blindside" revealed the story of Michael Oher, a young man who grew up on the wrong side of the tracks in Memphis. His life took a decidedly and dramatically different turn when he met a family that would love him, care for him, mentor him and, eventually, adopt him. Michael's status, and thus his identity, was forever changed. This story is a great picture of adoption and how it changes everything.

SESSION 7

If you're a follower of Jesus Christ you have a new identity and complete acceptance as a son, an heir. Not only has your Father removed and paid the penalty for your sins, but in Jesus Christ he gave you innumerable, countless blessings. Each of us should connect with and experience these blessing in our lives.

For far too long, many followers of Jesus have walked a road they didn't need to walk with a thousand things nipping at the heels of their souls. This road is oppressive and burdensome and disconnected from the grand and glorious truth of the gospel and causes believers to be unnecessarily tossed to and fro with hearts lacking confidence in God.

So, let's take a look at the next section of Galatians to see how we can leave these burdensome pathways of self-justification, anxiety and performance in order that we might find our feet firmly planted on the ground purchased by the death of Jesus.

GROUP NOTES:

SESSION 8

{ CATCH YOUR DRIFT WITH GOSPEL-CENTERED RELATIONSHIPS AND TEACHING. }

GALATIANS 4:8-31

⁸Formerly, when you did not know God, you were enslaved to those that by nature are not gods. ⁹But now that you have come to know God, or rather to be known by God, how can you turn back again to the weak and worthless elementary principles of the world, whose slaves you want to be once more? ¹⁰You observe days and months and seasons and years! ¹¹I am afraid I may have labored over you in vain.

¹²Brothers, I entreat you, become as I am, for I also have become as you are. You did me no wrong. ¹³You know it was because of a bodily ailment that I preached the gospel to you at first, ¹⁴and though my condition was a trial to you, you did not scorn or despise me, but received me as an angel of God, as Christ Jesus. ¹⁵What then has become of the blessing you felt? For I testify to you that, if possible, you would have gouged out your eyes and given them to me. ¹⁶Have I then become your enemy by telling you the truth? ¹⁷They make much of you, but for no good purpose. They want to shut you out, that you may make much of them. ¹⁸It is always good to be made much of for a good purpose, and not only when I am present with you, ¹⁹my little children, for whom I am again in the anguish of childbirth until Christ is formed in you! ²⁰I wish I could be present with you now and change my tone, for I am perplexed about you.

²¹Tell me, you who desire to be under the law, do you not listen to the law? ²²For it is written that Abraham had two sons, one by a slave woman and one by a free woman. ²³But the son of the slave was born according to the flesh, while the son of the free woman was born through promise. ²⁴Now this may be interpreted allegorically: these women are two covenants. One is from Mount Sinai, bearing children for slavery; she is Hagar. ²⁵Now Hagar is Mount Sinai in Arabia; she corresponds to the present Jerusalem,

SESSION 8 • Catch Your Drift with Gospel-Centered Relationships and Teaching.

for she is in slavery with her children. ²⁶But the Jerusalem above is free, and she is our mother. ²⁷For it is written,

"Rejoice, O barren one who does not bear;
break forth and cry aloud, you who are not in labor!
For the children of the desolate one will be more
than those of the one who has a husband."

²⁸Now you, brothers, like Isaac, are children of promise. ²⁹But just as at that time he who was born according to the flesh persecuted him who was born according to the Spirit, so also it is now. ³⁰But what does the Scripture say? "Cast out the slave woman and her son, for the son of the slave woman shall not inherit with the son of the free woman." ³¹So, brothers, we are not children of the slave but of the free woman.

REFLECTION:
Read through Galatians 4:8-31 at least three times this week. Each day make notes of any thoughts and observations and answer the questions provided.

DAY 1:
_____
_____
_____
_____
_____
_____

(vv. 8-9) Paul talks about the Galatians being slaves of what in these two verses?
_____
_____

DAY 2:
_____
_____
_____
_____
_____

(vv. 12-20) Apparently, Paul was ill when he first came to the Galatians. What words describe their relationship? _____

SESSION 8

DAY 3:

(vv. 21-27) Paul tells the Old Testament story of Abraham and his two sons. How is each described in these verses? _____

(vv. 28-31) Paul matches the "brothers" (followers of Jesus Christ) with Isaac. What words/phrases are used to describe Isaac's (and the brothers') identity? _____

GROUP READING: INTRODUCTION

People drift, we all do. Subtle forces in our life cause us to move toward behavior and ways of thinking that we never intend. We drift, for instance, from order to disorder. Just look at your garage. We drift when we give attention to the wrong thing. For example, when driving, you don't look into traffic coming toward you because you might drift into traffic. Or, when trying to stay debt free, you don't go visit the car lot full of new car smells, because you'll drift. The same thing goes for relationships. We drift in our marriages. We never intend for our love to stop growing, but if we don't give attention to what we need to give attention to, we drift away.

Today we will talk about a drift that we must catch because, if we don't, there is such a high cost on the soul. As a matter of fact, this is the most basic drift in all of the human soul and the focus of today's passage in Galatians.

GROUP NOTES:

SESSION 8 • Catch Your Drift with Gospel-Centered Relationships and Teaching.

Father:	Abraham	Abraham
Son:	Ishmael	Isaac
Mother:	Slave - Hagar	Free - Sarah
Covenants:	Law	Promise
Nations:	Arabians	Israelites
Jerusalem:	Earthly	Heavenly
Condition:	Bondage	Freedom

SESSION 9

{ THE WAY YOU EXPERIENCE GOD DETERMINES THE WAY PEOPLE EXPERIENCE YOU. }

GALATIANS 5:1-15

¹For freedom Christ has set us free; stand firm therefore, and do not submit again to a yoke of slavery.

²Look: I, Paul, say to you that if you accept circumcision, Christ will be of no advantage to you. ³I testify again to every man who accepts circumcision that he is obligated to keep the whole law. ⁴You are severed from Christ, you who would be justified by the law; you have fallen away from grace. ⁵For through the Spirit, by faith, we ourselves eagerly wait for the hope of righteousness. ⁶For in Christ Jesus neither circumcision nor uncircumcision counts for anything, but only faith working through love.

⁷You were running well. Who hindered you from obeying the truth? ⁸This persuasion is not from him who calls you. ⁹A little leaven leavens the whole lump. ¹⁰ I have confidence in the Lord that you will take no other view than mine, and the one who is troubling you will bear the penalty, whoever he is. ¹¹But if I, brothers, still preach circumcision, why am I still being persecuted? In that case the offense of the cross has been removed. ¹²I wish those who unsettle you would emasculate themselves!

¹³For you were called to freedom, brothers. Only do not use your freedom as an opportunity for the flesh, but through love serve one another. ¹⁴For the whole law is fulfilled in one word: "You shall love your neighbor as yourself." ¹⁵But if you bite and devour one another, watch out that you are not consumed by one another.

REFLECTION:

Read through Galatians 5:1-15 at least three times this week. Each day make notes of any thoughts and observations and answer the questions provided.

SESSION 9 • The Way You Experience God Determines the Way People Experience You.

DAY 1:

_____
_____
_____
_____
_____
_____

(v. 1) Paul restates his message or warning. What does he say Christ has done and what is the warning? _____
_____
_____

(vv. 2-4) Paul warns those who put on the yoke of slavery are in danger of what things happening? _____
_____
_____

DAY 2:

_____
_____
_____
_____
_____

(vv. 5-6) For what do we eagerly wait? In Christ Jesus neither circumcision nor uncircumcision counts for anything. What does? _____
_____
_____

DAY 3:

_____
_____
_____
_____
_____

(vv. 13-15) According to these verses, what is the purpose of our freedom?
_____
_____

GROUP READING: INTRODUCTION

There is a graphic at the bottom of this page that provides a metaphor, or a picture, for this entire passage. In the middle is the road we want to stay on, the "Way of Freedom," or the free way, and on each side of the free way is a ditch, the ditch of legalism and the ditch of license. The intention of this entire passage is that we would learn to walk in freedom, but what does this look like and what does it mean?

It means there is a freedom FROM and a freedom TO. We are free FROM trying to earn our way to God because we are free from the law and therefore free from being guilt-ridden by the law. We are also free from the bondage of our own sinful nature and living the destructive ways of our past. There is now no condemnation for those who are in Christ Jesus. We are free from the fear of death, free from so much.

But this passage is more about what we are free TO. What if you could live with an unselfish motivation, no longer make choices out of fear or self-interest or self-preservation or insecurities, and were free to really love with a reckless abandon kind of love?

What we're going to see in this passage is that we have this freedom that God gives us so we know how to love. If we experience God in a way that we have had his love lavished on our lives, then we're people others can experience and love. The way you and I experience God determines the way that people experience you and me. That's why we need this study today. We need to learn how we can stay on the free way and not get off into the ditch of legalism or the ditch of license. Those are not the paths that lead us to love. Let's take a look.

GROUP NOTES:

SESSION 10

{ BELIEF DETERMINES BEHAVIOR. }

GALATIANS 5:16-26

¹⁶But I say, walk by the Spirit, and you will not gratify the desires of the flesh. ¹⁷For the desires of the flesh are against the Spirit, and the desires of the Spirit are against the flesh, for these are opposed to each other, to keep you from doing the things you want to do. ¹⁸But if you are led by the Spirit, you are not under the law. ¹⁹Now the works of the flesh are evident: sexual immorality, impurity, sensuality, ²⁰idolatry, sorcery, enmity, strife, jealousy, fits of anger, rivalries, dissensions, divisions, ²¹envy, drunkenness, orgies, and things like these. I warn you, as I warned you before, that those who do such things will not inherit the kingdom of God. ²²But the fruit of the Spirit is love, joy, peace, patience, kindness, goodness, faithfulness, ²³gentleness, self-control; against such things there is no law. ²⁴And those who belong to Christ Jesus have crucified the flesh with its passions and desires.

²⁵If we live by the Spirit, let us also walk by the Spirit. ²⁶Let us not become conceited, provoking one another, envying one another.

REFLECTION:
Read through Galatians 5:16-26 at least three times this week. Each day make notes of any thoughts and observations and answer the questions provided.

SESSION 10 • Belief Determines Behavior.

DAY 1:

_____
_____
_____
_____
_____
_____

(v. 17) What are the two desires mentioned in these verses? _____
_____

DAY 2:

_____
_____
_____
_____
_____

(vv. 19-21) What are the works of the flesh as listed in the verses? _____
_____

DAY 3:

_____
_____
_____
_____
_____

(vv. 22-24) What is the fruit of the Spirit? _____
_____

GROUP READING: INTRODUCTION

Our behavior shows what is in our heart. If sins persistently plague us, it is either because we have never truly repented or we have repented but have not maintained that repentance. It's as if, having nailed our old nature to the cross, we keep wistfully returning to the scene of its execution. We begin to reach for it, caress it, long for it to return to us, and even try to take it down from the cross. We need to learn to leave it there. When some jealous, proud, malicious or impure thought enters our mind we must kick it out immediately. It is fatal and foolish to begin to toy with the idea of giving in to sin. We have declared war on sin and will not resume negotiations. We have crucified that flesh nature and will never consider removing the nails. And, if it is vital to be so ruthless in turning away from the things of the flesh, it is equally vital to be disciplined in turning toward the things of the Spirit.[a]

GROUP NOTES:

SESSION 10 • Belief Determines Behavior.

End Notes:
[a] The Bible Speaks Today: The Message of the Galatians, John R.W. Stott, Inter-Varsity Press, Leichester, England, Downers Grove, Illinois, U.S.A., 1986.

SESSION 11

{ HOW YOU SEE YOURSELF DETERMINES HOW YOU TREAT OTHERS. }

GALATIANS 5:26-6:5

²⁶Let us not become conceited, provoking one another, envying one another. ¹Brothers, if anyone is caught in any transgression, you who are spiritual should restore him in a spirit of gentleness. Keep watch on yourself, lest you too be tempted. ²Bear one another's burdens, and so fulfill the law of Christ. ³For if anyone thinks he is something, when he is nothing, he deceives himself. ⁴But let each one test his own work, and then his reason to boast will be in himself alone and not in his neighbor. ⁵For each will have to bear his own load.

REFLECTION:
Read through Galatians 5:26-6:5 at least three times this week. Each day make notes of any thoughts and observations and answer the questions provided.

DAY 1:
_____
_____
_____
_____
_____
_____

(vv. 5:26-6:1) These verses show a contrast in how we are to behave toward each other. What are the negative characteristics and what are the positive? What is the warning? _____
_____
_____
_____

SESSION 11 • How You See Yourself Determines How You Treat Others.

DAY 2:
_____
_____
_____
_____
_____

(vv. 6:2) What is it that fulfills the law of Christ? _____
_____
_____

DAY 3:
_____
_____
_____
_____
_____

(vv. 3-5) Circle each time the words "he" or "his" or "him" are used, then rewrite the verses replacing these words with your name. _____
_____
_____
_____
_____

GROUP READING:
We are almost to the end of Galatians and have seen all the contrasts of law-ridden religion with grace religion, or faith, and Paul said it comes to relationships. Relationships are affected by law and by grace. What you see in law-based homes, where it's all about the rules and checking boxes, is a need for acceptance by checking those boxes or you see anger and animosity. What does it look like when your life is based on the gospel, the good news of Jesus? What do "gospel relationships" look like? We're going to find the answers in our Scripture passage today. As we read, look for the big commandment about relationships.

GROUP NOTES:

SESSION 12

{ WE REAP WHAT WE SOW. }

GALATIANS 6:6-18

⁶One who is taught the word must share all good things with the one who teaches. ⁷Do not be deceived: God is not mocked, for whatever one sows, that will he also reap. ⁸For the one who sows to his own flesh will from the flesh reap corruption, but the one who sows to the Spirit will from the Spirit reap eternal life. ⁹And let us not grow weary of doing good, for in due season we will reap, if we do not give up. ¹⁰So then, as we have opportunity, let us do good to everyone, and especially to those who are of the household of faith.

¹¹See with what large letters I am writing to you with my own hand. ¹²It is those who want to make a good showing in the flesh who would force you to be circumcised, and only in order that they may not be persecuted for the cross of Christ. ¹³For even those who are circumcised do not themselves keep the law, but they desire to have you circumcised that they may boast in your flesh. ¹⁴But far be it from me to boast except in the cross of our Lord Jesus Christ, by which the world has been crucified to me, and I to the world. ¹⁵For neither circumcision counts for anything, nor uncircumcision, but a new creation. ¹⁶And as for all who walk by this rule, peace and mercy be upon them, and upon the Israel of God.

¹⁷From now on let no one cause me trouble, for I bear on my body the marks of Jesus.

¹⁸The grace of our Lord Jesus Christ be with your spirit, brothers. Amen.

REFLECTION:
Read through Galatians 6:6-18 at least three times this week. Each day make notes of any thoughts and observations and answer the questions provided.

SESSION 12 • We Reap What We Sow

DAY 1:

_____
_____
_____
_____
_____
_____

(v. 6) Who must share all good things with whom? _____
_____

DAY 2:

_____
_____
_____
_____
_____

(vv. 7-8) What does sowing to the flesh reap? What does sowing to the Spirit reap? _____
_____

DAY 3:

_____
_____
_____
_____
_____

(vv. 9-10) Paul acknowledges a difficulty in doing good, but he says we will reap if we do what? _____
_____

GROUP NOTES:

_____
_____
_____
_____

www.ingramcontent.com/pod-product-compliance
Lightning Source LLC
Chambersburg PA
CBHW061301040426
42444CB00010B/2457